shore

clay
matthews

shore

Cooper
Dillon

Acknowledgments:

Many thanks to my own wife, daughter, family, and friends. They are my light.

Additionally, I would like to thank Mark Issak for his extensive work collecting and summarizing Flood Stories from around the world. Without his work, this work would not be possible.

Finally, I would like to thank the editors of the following journals for publishing the noted selections:

    "Act Two" – *Guernica*
    "Act Three" – *diode*

Copyright © 2016 by Clay Matthews
All rights reserved
First edition

Cooper Dillon Books
San Diego, California
CooperDillon.com

Cover Design by Max Xiantu

ISBN-13: 978-1-943899-00-5

Printed in the United States

Contents

Prologue 1
    Act One 3
Chorus 9
    Act Two 10
Chorus 18
    Act Three 20
Chorus 26
    Act Four 28
Chorus 36
    Act Five 39
Epilogue 49
    Notes 52

I love water, I *love* water —

but I also love air, and fire.

>   from "The Birds" by Robert Creeley

Prologue

Listen: a story begins here:
a coming flood, a man
sitting on a bucket

with a fishing pole
and 40 oz., some shadow
with a guitar in the clouds

singing *Mean old levee, taught me*
to weep and moan. A louse
and a flea kept house together

and brewed beer
in an egg-shell.
The things that happen

before the thing
that is going to happen.
Before the flood, the carp

flew out of the river
and made rainbows.
In an older story

the colors don't come
until the end.
The little house has burnt herself —

a shot-gun duplex in flames
at the water's edge.
The tree shook

its leaves and a little girl
came with a pitcher.
A man whistled

at a woman in a window,
the turning of chrome rims
wrote the sun's lament

into asphalt.
The end of the story
is that everything drowned

together. The shadow sang
Listen: nothing
is quiet as water.

Act One

People once lived forever
and knew no troubles.
A long song on a bird's wing —

the brake lights of a Cadillac
driving away. *How shall we sing
the Lord's song in a strange land?*

A god skipped a stone
and the stone
became a woman. A woman

became a man. A man
became a city
of liquor stores and lottery tickets.

Why did the clouds
follow them? Her mother's bones
in a china cup —

there by the river
they wept when they remembered
darkness and children

playing ball
under the streetlight,
the boldest daughter

cutting heaven
into paper snowflakes.
Somewhere someone

must have done somebody
wrong. Somewhere
they kept calling

for rain. Our water began
outside someone else's kitchen.
Chicken on the grill,

lightning striking a cow
stone dead. Omens
in the cornbread batter—

a little preacher in a blue suit
told her *Gret God can save!*
But all she could hear

was thunder.
What made them wicked
one way or the other—

the eight ball or the crow's
feet, the lace curtains
yellowed by the sun?

In the parking lot,
Christian children filled
sandbags. In the grocery stores

people flooded the aisles
for white bread
and ground beef,

the offered tears
of onions and strong drink.
When God told Abraham

to kill a son, was *Yes, Lord*
really the answer
he wanted to hear?

We've been translated
to walk amongst the birds
and willows. She was a wife

but they could not call her
Falsehood or Misfortune.
Once, children were born

and could command
the sun and moon.
In the kitchen first

she was angry at nothing
in particular
while she drowned

her dishes in the sink.
The little engine
of his jon boat. Bluegill

cooked over hot coals
at the water's edge.
Before this,

before these people,
there was a land
of no barren women,

no stillbirth.
But what comes
next? Even the gods

grew hungry by the fire.
Even the gods
were frightened once.

Write a history
and bury it. Tomorrow
a woman will read it

in seashells and beer
bottles, the river lapping
at the hem

of her gown. She was clothed
with the sun sometimes,
perfumed by lavender

and horse. He remembered her
before the flood as she would
remember him after,

as children singing
a song in rounds:
life is but a dream.

Words as tributaries,
pages as promise.
If you follow me, they read,

I will make you fishers of men.
She took her devotional
there by the window

with coffee. *To beat the sunrise,*
he said, leaving
with his thermos and tackle box.

A brother and sister
in every story. A husband
and wife with a hoe-handle

in a clay pot.
We were all relatives
once. The urns on the mantle

the children were told
never to touch. Ashes
or the ocean?

The sound of water
running inside a tree.
One day the bald cardinal

stopped coming back
to the feeder. A prophecy
in gold teeth. In darkness

he wound and unwound
the trotline. In darkness
the catfish grew

like the sound
of heartbeats, her ear
on his chest, the smell

of mint and malt liquor
on his breath.
The crow who returned

with a birch twig.
The black oil
sunflower spilling

from the feeder.
She was a long time
spent watching the trees

outside the window,
looking at a world divided
by pillows and flannel sheets.

Among other things,
he taught his friends
to make strong liquor —

a tea kettle and copper pipe,
a mash turning sour
in the old white bucket.

There was a man
they heard tell
told a story

and turned
to stone. A rooster
sits forever

on his shoulder
and crows, all around
starlings scatter like seeds.

Chorus

He was afraid to live. She was afraid

of him dying. The king of the water demons fell

in love with the woman. Sky and earth

longed for souls and bones. Sibling children.

Grown lovers. They stood as the tap water ran,

thirsty. We descend from wooden sculptures.

We descend from the trees. The roots run

to the foundation. The water follows

the roots. If there was a child, it was squalling.

If there was a bird, it sang to the coming

flood. The river rinsed them. The fire forged them.

Early one morning, the stereo turned,

water was comin' in my door.

Act Two

Curse the rain, he thought. Curse the repetition, the weatherman, the dead dog and the other in his house, the roosters on the back stoop, the bottle, the snuff tin, the sho' nuff', the rice fields and levies, the thunder, the boat, the trolley motor, the carp and the catfish, the long bridge and the long highway, the nightgown and the toothbrush, the never stopping, the never knowing, curse the never never coming. Under the porch the black ants carried the scraps away. They were leaving— everything was leaving. The hawk on the highway who had sat on that powerline for years, the neighbors in their old sedan, the news crew who had asked him

What are you most afraid of losing? and *Tell us about floods* and *Have you ever*

stood on a hilltop and seen the world end? He cleaned the charcoal off his hands,

the motor oil, the grease, he cleaned the chicken shit and the mud,

the fish scales and the blood, everything water, everything rinsed, everything

in a half of a house that leant to the sun in the west, everything

in a rusted bicycle and his old truck on blocks, everything in the coop

and the crutches laid against the wall of the shed. Some nights

when he held her he held everything. Some nights the windows

seemed so far away. Some nights like Jacob he wrestled with God —

I could murder a man, he thought some nights, but he could never make out

that man's face. He was not blessed. He was not broken, either.

The tooth he lost and planted with a plum tree. The plum tree bearing fruit,

the empty canning jars in the pantry, her hands rubbing balm

on his bad hip in the morning, another bad tooth aching, he dreamt of taking

his heart out and pushing it down the disposal, down the sewer,

down the unknown, down deep to where he couldn't hear it beat

in the darkness. A pile of broken turtle shells and a soup on the stove.

Born as a fleshball, he thought, *destined for worms*. He did more damage

to fish fried whole than the sun does to a dead carcass, than time does

to a dead carcass in the sun, he was thinking these days of the sun and of time and carcasses, they had wandered off somewhere with the cat.

A beautiful umbrella. Something he'd wanted always to buy her. An umbrella

she could fly on, an umbrella she could sleep under, an umbrella

he could lay down over the water and make a bridge. He looked at the chicken bones

on his plate and knew something bad was coming. The stench

of the garbage before garbage day, of the water before the river crests.

From the book of Micah: *Enemy, don't laugh at me. I have fallen,*

but I will get up again. I sit in the shadow of trouble now, but the Lord will be a light

for me. June evenings with a frog gig and a bucket. The eyes

of something that can't stop staring into the white. To return from the dead:

13

the fish on the stringer going slowly still until they meet the shore,

animals destined for air, men destined for one last gilled breath

and then moss and driftwood. The filet knife through the belly

of a pregnant snake, the millet and corn in the throat of a turtle dove.

Talk of marriage, and then marriage. They were uncertain

so she asked the sun as it rose in the morning. *Yes, Lord*, he said to the old blanket

they fought over at nights. *Yes, Lord* to the chicken thigh and the Styrofoam

full of worms, the cricket cage, the leaking rivets of the boat, the first light

hitting the water like foiled gold, yes to the gold tooth, the pocket knife

rusting on the nightstand beside the bed, yes bed, yes night, *Yes forever*

he said instead of *I do*, something not right about the personal pronouns in a world of white lace and Sunday dinners and cracked engine blocks and floods. *The ground we stand on is merely a skin covering an abyss of water.* An old man digging in a river bed to find its soul. The first time she miscarried he rocked her for two days. The second time he cried alone in his boat and let all his catch go free. The tears of god: who would know any better about the rain? A struggle between a snake and a higher power. The stones he let walk on water. He dreamed of his mother saved from what was below—her hair caught in the branches of a locust tree. She knocked on his head and he woke up. Something was already frying in the pan. A pregnant woman and a pregnant snake.

15

A pig trough full of scales and rice. He wondered how it all balanced out—the good and the bad, the nights and the mornings, the hook in the eye of a fish versus the hook in the mouth, the scales of time as golden as the bluegill passing from the darkness to light, the darkness and the light, the darkness and the water, the water and sleep, his hands and the things his hands had touched. The Cottonwoods sometimes covered the backwaters in white. The leaves of a tree repopulating the world with corpses. The way fish guts sometimes reminded him of menstrual blood, the way she bled, the way she was created to bleed. He stared a long time into his coffee and knew he had created nothing. *Nothing will come of nothing.* Of course it was a father

who said that. He heard the bees whispering: *water*.
He heard the flies whispering: *nothing*. He was born in a tantrum
of curse words and tears. Only a flood could drown out
the light he still held inside. Only a crow on a branch looking west
and then leaving him. *All that's left*, he thought, but it was too much
to hold with his hands.

Chorus

The line disappears
into water. The line goes under,
the line breaks.

They became like rocks.
On each other
they cast a spell.

Maybe the right words
but the wrong bird's beak.
Maybe the wrong breath

but the right circle.
Wedding bands and a jar
of honey. His side

of the bed and hers.
They lined up in the morning
for the sun.

In the evenings
they lined their bodies
like canned fish. They lined

the walls with paintings
of trees and photographs
of the past.

In line for what
was coming. In line to hear
a man sing

about rain. The line
disappears into water.
The line goes under,

the line breaks.

Act Three

Childless in a world
full of children.
A tobacco plug

and hibiscus tea.
Six sisters and a mother
who darkened her door

no more. In the streets
a man dressed
as a dead president

handing out tax
flyers. In her dreams
a baby drowned

in honey. *All the people
turned into birds.*
The needle and the thread.

The crochet hook
and the weight of that word,
mend. *To mend*, she thought,

but she felt tragic
sometimes the way
our reflections

come out of nowhere
in storefront windows
and leaded glass.

She was not
concentrating. She watched
him outside

urinating on the Queen
Anne's lace and singing.
At the river's edge,

when the water rose
to her feet, or she
walked out further,

she was changed
like a bird is changed,
the baby cardinals

putting on color
at last, at last the Ugly
Duckling crying:

I will fly away to them.
Lines of water
and land, sun

and trees, the dog
fetching sticks,
no man moved me —

till the Tide...
The way the fish
came up to clean

the meat off
a chicken bone.
That fish she saw

alone one morning,
that whale of a fish,
the big treble hook

he pulled from a drawer
after she told him.
She felt betrayed

and loved that he
listened all at once.
She felt the rim

of the china cup
and read from the book
of John: *Now is your time*

of grief, but I will see you
again and you will rejoice,
and no one

will take away your joy.
The way that back door
closed like god

was closing up shop
forever. *Gone fishin',*
she thought,

and never forgave
herself for laughing.
The moment and all

the years. The days
and days punctuated
by men begging

for spare change
and an angle from which
better to see her,

the lines of the grocery
store, the lines
cashing checks, the lines

running electricity
from her house
to the power company,

from the power company
to the train station,
from the train station

to wherever it was
the great big world
went out there.

The lines of cars
leaving town.
At night the stars

looked down on her
like eyes. She felt
watched, and embarrassed,

and safe. She felt
softest sometimes
alone with the crickets

and a bottle of beer.
Was the hope drunk?
She wondered

if the mosquitoes
would bleed her out.
Bloodletting, she thought,

her life a stained glass
of giving and red;
she wanted to drop

a leaf on the water
and sail away.
Life was not a prison

but she counted
walls, quietly in this boat
of fools and deaf mutes.

Some days she felt
he took the best
of everything.

How she looked forward
to his return.
She was the battle

between fire and water,
born of the drippings
from stalactites

and candles, the wet
match-box drying
on the counter.

At night she dreamt
of her hair held beautifully
with fish hooks, adorned

in thistle. At night
she poured the sea
from her head,

an ocean taken
with its own image
of oceans.

The news was nothing
new. Through her gold–hoop
earrings she watched

the rain turn heavy,
and she felt herself
a heavy drop

and wanted only then
to fit through
such a small circle

and be somewhere
else, to grow
small enough

the wind
would permit her
flight.

Chorus

The Raven assumed wings.

    The Wise Man placed mud

on the water, and breathed

    on it, making it grow.

In the fog, in the darkness,

    he thought he heard an infant

on the other end of his boat,

    clearing his path

through the billows.

    Where is the first man

to build a canoe?

    Where is the Raven

begging not to be cast down

    into the deeps?

A tree for a wife.

A song for a promise.

Her in her kerchief,

    he in his cap.

Wilt thou not chase the white whale?

    The best bait

for a big fish

    he knew

was a smaller fish.

    The valleys and mountains.

In a clearing he saw

    two moons,

and, not knowing

    which one was real,

followed the brighter.

Act Four

The water kept rising, following the woman. Born of another woman

who had no husband, he wondered if the dream of a child were real,

if the story of a fish sent to swallow a man would ever come true again,

was his lot already cast? A fish to ride to forever on.

A fish to spit him out on the shore, a tree to grow there and shade him, a tree

for the worms to eat. From the book of Jonah:

So they took up Jonah, and cast him forth into the sea: and the sea ceased

from her raging. A monster in the river where the river grew into something larger, older, a darkness and something that called to him: *fish,*

leviathan. A commandment or a catalogue, the nouns of god,

a catfish as old as the cypress roots under water, making a smile of his whiskers

with pomade, the mirror of sky he looks up to from below.

Stars and shadows ain't good to see by. If time had created him and this fish,

if time had created the hook or if time was the hook, if time distant

bent toward him like the moonlight: *Holding all I used to be sorry about*

like the new moon holding water. A fishing line like a rope of arrows

from the clouds to the water, the musical score of the treble

hook, the fight of something caught, violent and beautiful and short-lived

and eternal and fishing, he thought, must be one of our oldest metaphors, dying, he thought, must be one of our oldest lies,

time, he thought, must exist on a string between reel, rod, and whatever pulls

away below. A fish he had no intentions of eating.

A fish he had no intentions of throwing back.

I have spread my dreams under your feet. A promise he had made

to himself once as a child, a promise before her, a promise before liquor

and time cards, before heaven and the lottery, a promise before

he had given up on promises, a child he was promising then

to catch a monster, just a boy with no father who wanted

to pull something back. He put on the years like cornmeal batter, time had made him a fried shell of what once swam underneath. Long ago,

the people became so numerous they ate all of the fish

then started to eat each other. But he was alone now

with this water, rising in this darkness broken by light through the sky,

broken again by the ripples of time.

There is a road, no simple highway, between the dawn and the dark of night.

Here in this boat, he wept once for five days. Blindly he reached

for something to hold and grasped the long branches of a willow.

He always found his way home through her hair,

the brush on the nightstand, the curls from humidity on her forehead,

31

the forever of a long lock cut and ribboned, marking a page

from the book of Song of Solomon: *Set me as a seal upon your heart,*

as a seal upon your arm, for love is as strong as death.

The way the goodbye was not right that morning, the way the goodbyes

are never right. Here in this boat, pouring shots of liquor into his coffee,

he sang a song about letting his light shine forever, he shed his clothes

and dove into the water. Never had he felt so far away

from earth. Never had the cold mud of the bottom been this unreachable,

as mysterious and dark and malleable as it were, never had he not known

what he was not. What is the right dream now?

Now that she was so far away, now that he knew what the end was, the way catfish taste the world through their skin, and breathe,

the way right and wrong rocked like either end of this boat. Which end

was he rocked on? *We were together. I forget the rest.*

His soul sent to the moon in a gossamer balloon, fastened

to the earth by a long rope. Now surrounded by water he knew

it was always water already: *We are two fishes swimming in the sea together.*

He dreamed of a child born on a mountaintop, laurel

and rhododendron blossoming, a fire and the waters bowing to the hem

of her skirt, breastmilk and a song she was singing

between rusted washing machines and dogs howling, he was waking up

from some long sleep and getting tired all at once,

he thought he saw a coyote beating a rug against an oak tree, making fog.

Two feathers the coyote laid side by side. In the morning

they became a man and a woman. A bird's wing caught on a stick.

Maybe the first thing ever created in the world was a flower.

Long ago, an old woman, jealous of the bird's power, came with her basket

carrying the sea, and poured it out until she covered the land.

The error bred in the bone... Not universal love/ But to be loved alone.

In this dream he was a bird planting feathers that turned

into children. In this dream she was the mother of them all.

He heard a story on the radio once that time was relative,

and he knew then that everything was relative, and this made him

not afraid, but family, the familiar darkness and light

bending around the bow of his boat. Because the raven did not return,

it was changed from white to black.

Because he saw the leviathan at dawn, they were changed to brothers

and traded bodies. Each wailed when they lost the other,

his footprints leading from the water, the wake of his giant body swimming

away. When a catfish dies, he sinks. When a human dies, he floats.

When nothing dies they become the stars together and are reborn

in a place without time, a place where we rock on the edge of everything

like a bobber with nothing on the hook, no man to cast it out

or reel it in. *The problem with shores*, he thought.

The promise of shores, he thought.

Chorus

Have you grieved,
dear Reader? Have you lost
something, missed

something, misplaced
the better parts
of your heart?

Has the ghost
of time picked
these things up

and moved them
in your house?
What do you know

of one-hundred years
hence? What is the pang
that cuts at you

from childhood, years
gone — the years, oh,
have they sped away?

For a long time,
she travelled, having forgotten
about her anger.

But one day
she happened
to remember,

and sat crying.
The people were meant
to live forever,

but he wasn't invited.
Now we all
must travel this road

to the other world.
In the beginning
of time, in September.

She was born, she bled,
she grew older,
she mourned

her image in the water.
What has god offered us,
in pity? Day

after day, the dog
stood at the river bank
and howled.

For a sign
that he spoke the truth,
the dog revealed

the back of his neck,
which was raw
and bare

showing flesh and bone.
The little water
monsters, her children,

wailed, too.
A small cardinal
brought fire from heaven

again. She burned
everywhere inside.
A man who could see

the future told her
to plant a hollow reed
and run. She found

the car keys
where they should not
have been.

She watched
the smoke pouring out
the windows

before she parted,
leaving almost everything
as it was.

Act Five

A book of matches
and a music box.
An old man

in the park
playing basketball
with a ghost.

Everyone was gone.
The quiet
of empty doorways

and the long stretch
of road going
either way.

He had not come
home. Three days
gone and never

this long, she watched
a barn swallow
writing some language

she could not see
in the sky, she turned
to the white face

of the wind
and wished to blossom
into a bird.

Once, people
were able to travel
by looking where

they wanted to go,
and then
they were there.

This house.
This half
of a house, the memories

that settled
on the floor
like the dog's shed hair,

the spider
who built her web
in the kitchen window,

wove a golden egg,
had children,
and went away

as we often do
to die. Memories
like a sack full

of stars someone
had spilled
on the floor,

the way they shone
in the morning light.
Memories like the clothes

in his closet,
his dirty undershirts
in the hamper—

You cannot fold a Flood—
And put it in a drawer—
His name

as she had created it
from bits of her heart.
She had wondered

about his going,
and now his being
gone. She had wondered

if she might fly,
if she might cast a net
in the sky

and pull down
his face in the moon,
and be free.

A bird who makes
a nest
from her own down.

A bird with a song
that tells the story
of the great mystery.

Gone, gone, gone,
gone. She felt nothing
but an anchor

pulling her, holding her,
cast iron sunk deep
in the dark bottom

of the water,
she was not
free, she was

weeping, she was not
weeping, she was
bawling — there are no verbs

for what she was
or is, she was a heart
that held another heart

in this house, a hand
rubbing balm, lips
kissing away trouble

from his dark neck,
the morning, who
could say

what a violent thing
daybreak is?
Yesterday, after

another storm
she saw two rainbows.
One, she thought

to be god's promise,
but who was promising
with the other,

and what? She stood
at the water's edge
waiting, waves lapped

at her hem. The rocks
were so soft
her feet sank

into them. How long
ago was it
they planted a garden,

slept and dreamed
and harvested?
That tree they cut

down in the yard.
That tree now grown
back overnight.

She was the dog
who took off its skin
to become a woman

and do the work.
She was the dishes
and broom,

the soap and the faucet,
the bed she no longer
slept in, the bed

she no longer made.
She opened
a bottle of beer

and wondered
if the sun
had ever lost someone,

if the light
had ever left
something completely

to the darkness.
After the dog
took off its skin,

the man burned the pelt
to keep her from turning
back into a dog again.

She needed
to burn now.
She needed

these memories
to be a lantern.
She poured kerosene

over everything—
the necklace
he gave her, the ring,

the flower vases,
the bible, the bed,
the refrigerator,

the coffee cups,
her nightgown,
the welcome mat,

the porch, the irises,
and into the water
pooling

on the walkway.
She threw one match
for herself,

and one match
for his memory.
She held another

until it burned
her fingers,
and threw it

for the future
because
she desperately

needed light.
You cannot put a Fire out—
A Thing that can ignite....

She knew he was
dead. Had he
ascended? Had he

sunk? She vomited
in the tall grass
and glowed.

The flames
rose like a hand
reaching out,

and in the blaze
she saw
his face.

We're born dumb,
she thought, until
a dove

from a lofty tree
gives us language,
so many languages

we can't understand
each other.
But love,

she thought.
But love.
She had prayed

for light, and light
appeared. All her children
became flowers

when they jumped
from the fire
to where the stars are.

You cannot fold a Flood—
And put it in a drawer—
The wooden people,

she thought, have nothing
in their hearts.
She removed

her clothes
and bathed once more
in the water.

There is something
like electricity
that reaches out

and holds us
when we're needing
held. In the water

she felt him
all over her.
She cut off

a small piece
of her ear
and buried it

where once
the garden was.
So much water,

she thought,
we will never
say goodbye.

She dressed,
still wet, and climbed
into the car

and drove east.
She felt him
in the steering wheel,

in the water dripping
from her hair,
in her tears.

But love, she thought.
And in her belly
something grew.

Epilogue

When he died,
the rain stopped.
Or else, the water

saw a great fire, bowed,
and withdrew.
She bore twins

on a mountaintop
and named them
Father and Mother.

Life returned
to life — music blaring
from stereos,

televisions forecasting
sunny weather.
Boats were sent out

into the water, people
skied and drank
and burned, vultures

and crows cleaned
the dead. Stars shone
all through the night.

You see,
the oldest love story,
between the sun

and the moon,
never ends.
Once upon a time,

people didn't die —
they just slept awhile,
and woke refreshed

with embered fragments
of a beautiful dream
fading from their mind.

Once upon a time,
he brought her
a stringer of fish

and she offered him
a drink. They had dreamed
together, and loved

the smaller parts
of their days. They had sat
at the kitchen table

with their eyes closed
and hoped.
These are our stories,

and who's to say
what's true?
Even now, people are building

their houses on the water,
so that when the water rises,
they may rise with it.

Notes

References to Flood Stories throughout were all taken from Mark Isaak's wonderful work "Flood Stories from Around the World." Isaak has catalogued and summarized an exhaustive group of Flood Stories, which are available online and include references to the original source material. Lines from his summaries have been summarized and/or integrated directly into this book, loosely in the tradition of the cento (lines here are used more sparingly and blended into the larger verse narrative). Additionally, other lines from songs, poems, stories, and etc. have been utilized as well. The notes follow, referencing each section individually.

The "Prologue" contains lines from Kansas Joe McCoy and Memphis Minnie's "When the Levee Breaks" and The Brothers Grimm's "Little Louse and Little Flea."

"Act One" contains lines from Psalm 137:1, the Transylvanian Gypsy Flood Story, the Hebrew Flood Story, "Row, Row, Row Your Boat," the Chaldean Flood Story, Matthew 4:19, the Cameroon Flood Story, the Altaic Flood Story, the Tuvinian Flood Story, and the Mongolia Flood Story.

The First "Chorus" contains lines from the Lushai (Assam) Flood Story, the Lisu Flood Story, the Lolo Flood Story, and Big Bill Broonzy's "Southern Flood Blues."

"Act Two" contains lines from the Zhuang Flood Story, Micah 7:8-10, the Benua-Jakun Flood Story, the Ifugao Flood Story, and Shakespeare's King Lear.

"Act Three" contains lines from the Manger Flood Story, the New Hebrides Flood Story, the Mangaia (Cook Islands) Flood Story, the Hawaii Flood Story, Hans Christian Andersen's "The Ugly Duckling," Emily Dickinson's "I Started Early – Took My Dog," John 16:22, and Shakespeare's MacBeth 1:7:512.

The Third "Chorus" contains lines from the Tlingit (southern Alaska coast) Flood Story, the Hareskin (Alaska) Flood Story, the Tinneh (Alaska and south) Flood Story, the Loucheux (Dindjie) (a Tinneh Tribe, Alaska) Flood story, the Thompson Indians (British Columbia) Flood Story, Herman Melville's Moby Dick, and Clement Clark Moore's "A Visit from St. Nicholas."

"Act Four" contains lines lines from the Haida (Queen Charlotte Is., British Columbia) Flood Story, the Skokomish (Washington) Flood Story, the Nisqually (Washinginton) Flood Story, the Smith River (northern California coast) Flood Story, the Tuleyome Miwok (near Clear Lake, California) Flood Story, the Salinan (California) Flood Story, the Ashochimi (California) Flood Story, the Cree (Canada) Flood Story, the Chippewa (Ojibway) (Ontario, Minnesota, Wisconsin) Flood Story, Jonah 1:15, Song of Solomon 8:6, Mark Twain's The Adventures of Huckleberry Finn, William Faulkner's The Sound and the Fury, W.B. Yeats's "Aedh wishes for the Cloths of Heaven," The Grateful Dead's "Ripple," a variation of Walt Whitman's "Once I Pass'd Through a Populous City," Walt Whitman's "We Two, How Long We Were Fool'd," and W. H. Auden's "September 1, 1939."

The Fourth "Chorus" contains lines from the Chippewa (Ojibdway) (Ontario, Minnesota, Wisconsin) Flood Story, the Cherokee (Great Lakes area; eastern Tennessee), the Mandand (North Dakota) Flood Story, the Natchez (Lower Mississippi) Flood Story, and the Caddo (Oklahoma, Arkansas) Flood Story.

"Act Five" contains lines from the Jicarilla Apache (northeastern New Mexico) Flood Story, the Sia Flood Story, the Pima (southwest Arizona) Flood Story, the Tarahumara (Northern Mexico) Flood Story, the Huichol (western Mexico) Flood Story, the Tepecano (southeast of Huichols) Flood Story, the Nahua (central Mexico) Flood Story, the Totonac (eastern Mexico) Flood Story, the Quiché (Guatemala) Flood Story, and Emily Dickinson's "You cannot put a Fire out—."

The "Epilogue" contains lines from the Komililo Nandi Flood Story, the Selk'nam (southern tip of Argentina) Flood Story, the Pamary, Abedery, and the Kataushy (Purus R., Brazil) Flood Story.

Clay Matthews is the author of *Superfecta* (Ghost Raod Press), *Runoff* (BlazeVOX [books]). *Pretty, Rooster (*Cooper Dillon Books) and two chapbooks: *Muffler* (H_NGM_N B_ _KS) and *Western Reruns* (End & Shelf Books). He lives in Greeneville, Tennessee. Visit his blog at claymatthews.blogspot.com.

www.ingramcontent.com/pod-product-compliance
Lightning Source LLC
Chambersburg PA
CBHW021452080526
44588CB00009B/805